T0067435

THE SICKNESS OF
EFFORT

GARY BRYANT

BALBOA.
PRESS

A DIVISION OF HAY HOUSE

Copyright © 2016 Gary Bryant.

All rights reserved. No part of this book may be used or reproduced by any means, graphic, electronic, or mechanical, including photocopying, recording, taping or by any information storage retrieval system without the written permission of the author except in the case of brief quotations embodied in critical articles and reviews.

Balboa Press books may be ordered through booksellers or by contacting:

Balboa Press
A Division of Hay House
1663 Liberty Drive
Bloomington, IN 47403
www.balboapress.com
1 (877) 407-4847

Because of the dynamic nature of the Internet, any web addresses or links contained in this book may have changed since publication and may no longer be valid. The views expressed in this work are solely those of the author and do not necessarily reflect the views of the publisher, and the publisher hereby disclaims any responsibility for them.

The author of this book does not dispense medical advice or prescribe the use of any technique as a form of treatment for physical, emotional, or medical problems without the advice of a physician, either directly or indirectly. The intent of the author is only to offer information of a general nature to help you in your quest for emotional and spiritual well-being. In the event you use any of the information in this book for yourself, which is your constitutional right, the author and the publisher assume no responsibility for your actions.

Any people depicted in stock imagery provided by Thinkstock are models, and such images are being used for illustrative purposes only. Certain stock imagery © Thinkstock.

Print information available on the last page.

ISBN: 978-1-5043-6165-1 (sc)
ISBN: 978-1-5043-6166-8 (e)

Balboa Press rev. date: 07/19/2016

TABLE OF CONTENTS

PREFACE

The question of effort is one that cuts across all spiritual traditions, ancient, medieval, modern, and contemporary or postmodern. It is one of the most effective of "skillful means," or ways to help those who enter a spiritual way or path to transition from the conditioning with which they negotiate consensus reality to a new way of being in the world. Yet it is also one of the most misunderstood ways, partly because the transition itself is so difficult, strewn with obstacles and completely counterintuitive to a lifetime of familial and societal learning.

We are taught to make efforts in order to attain valued aims or goals, and we formulate objectives that need to be met along the way. We feel the need to obtain something, and, given the inextricable connection between need and value, we value what we believe will meet our need. What we learn about the place of effort in all this is that we need to assert ourselves, to take whatever action is required to attain our objectives and eventually attain our goal. Somehow our identities, our feeling or sense of whom we are and what we can do, are deeply involved in these efforts.

The primary objective of a spiritual path or way is to challenge this usually unquestioned process, to upend the entire conditioning that reinforces this way of being and living, and in so doing change the very meaning of effort. Effort, in ordinary life, connotes a tense doing by an agent of change; effort in more advanced stages of spiritual life dispenses with tension, doing, and agency as all these are understood and accepted by the holding culture. In this regard a spiritual way is profoundly countercultural.

Using a medical metaphor for emphasis, a spiritual or inner way of working or doing considers the usual understanding of effort as a kind of sickness, a pathology that is bound up with the larger cultural malady which leads us astray at every turn, convincing us that we have a unity and continuity that in reality does not obtain. A given path or way intends to wean us from the usual notion of effort by instilling in us a sane, enlightened view of effort.

After an initial exploration of the process of effort in its usual sense, several chapters follow in which we will explore how several important spiritual traditions both introduce effort and assist aspirants in its reevaluation. A concluding chapter will then present an enlightened approach to effort, using as examples the cases explored in previous chapters.

In so doing we will see how effective spiritual ways can retain the idea that we do have an indispensable part to play in the drama of inner growth or evolution, while rejecting the unhelpful and even self-destructive idea that in order to engage a spiritual way we must do nothing. This is an advanced teaching that can be safely introduced only after considerable experience in a given spiritual tradition; the undermining of our habitual way of making efforts is a subtle process that usually requires many years of guidance, and cannot be directly delivered to inexperienced aspirants without serious risk of confusion and discouragement. The disastrous approaches of such confused and confusing teachings like Neoadvaita are best avoided by those who embark on a spiritual way of transformation, for an effective translation, a new way of conceiving oneself and the world, must precede transformation for the vast majority of self-identified "seekers."

CHAPTER ONE

INTRODUCTION

Effort and Struggle

All spiritual ways of liberation begin with the necessity of effort, of a struggle with one's ordinary way of thinking, feeling, and sensing oneself. Those who attempt to engage the process of liberation in any other way will soon abandon the process as futile, literally senseless.

What is not understood by the nascent aspirant, and what is understood by elders in a given path or way, is that one's conception of effort is contaminated by one's overall conditioning inculcated by family and society, forming an essential part of that conditioning, and from which one will eventually be liberated.

One can only begin from where one is, working with one's current understanding. It is inevitable, then, that when one is told to struggle, make effort, one will engage the process of liberation with a mistaken sense and feeling not only of effort but also of oneself.

Struggle With The Mind

All authentic spiritual traditions demand that aspirants struggle with the contents of the mind, with ordinary thought. For one's usual thoughts, orbiting and reinforcing as they do a mistaken sense and feeling of identity, form the major obstacle to an authentic feeling of oneself.

A given tradition, then, will introduce the idea that one's thought life, formerly experienced as one's ownmost identity, can actually be made into an object of observation, and that senior to one's thoughts is a more active attention that can watch or observe the arising and passing away of ordinary thoughts. And that such thinking, far from comprising one's identity, is only *about* this supposed identity.

Another struggle that involves the mind is the effort to attain an intellectual understanding of the ideas that support the practices of a given way. Through reading, discussion, individual and group pondering, one attempts to attain enough intellectual knowledge to proceed to the more practical applications of the ideas. A distinction arises between one's habitual ideas and the sacred ideas presented for one's serious consideration. An understanding emerges about the necessity to master a way's ideas, first intellectually, then, eventually, on a practical, experiential level.

The Somatic Struggle

Authentic spiritual ways also demand that sufficient attention be given to one's somatic structure, to the body, in ways that are novel and that usually obtain in periods of meditation or contemplation. Functions and features of the body that are usually ignored or overlooked are brought into awareness, the best and most obvious example being the breath.

The effort to attend the breath – say, during a period of seated meditation – is initially experienced as a daunting task. One's attention is continually distracted from the object of attention, and one is instructed to bring it back to the breath as soon as one realizes it has wandered. Complicating this fact are the thoughts that comment on this distraction; these thoughts are usually negative judgments about one's inability to remain with the breathing. An additional effort, then, is needed to observe such judgments without further judgment about the judgments. Because one can only begin with one's current understanding of effort or struggle, the understanding obtained from a lifetime of conditioning, the effort both to attend the breath and one's commentary can be a prime source of further struggle.

The Struggle for Feeling

The process of liberation offered by a given spiritual way involves a growth of feeling, primarily a feeling of Being. The effort or struggle to engage this process of growth must contend with ordinary feeling: one's usual emotions, reactions, and above all one's usual feeling of self.

In addition, one enters a spiritual path unaware that one's thought life is enslaved by the process of desire, which is an unconscious identification of Self-energy with an impulse to meet a given need. Aside from the *process* of desire, an individual desire can be more, or less, a faithful expression of the originating need. By and large, our desires are distant and distorted echoes of a real need, and in fulfilling the desire the need remains unmet. No better example of this unmet need is the ontological need, the need for Being, for this need is almost always left languishing as we pursue substitute objects of desire.

The Struggle With And For Identity

The principal struggle is with one's socially conditioned sense of self and identity and for one's authentic Identity. The appearance of two sorts of effort is seductive and ultimately obstructive; the struggle with the old and for the new constitutes a single effort.

To weaken the old one must strengthen the new; to strengthen the new one must weaken the old. Development of the new depends upon withdrawing the energy of the life-force from the old. Once this withdrawal begins, space also begins to open, inviting the advent of an even more active force, the force or energy of Being itself, which is the essential food for the new feeling of Self.

The struggle with the old and for the new is the most daunting of all efforts, for it challenges all the thoughts, feelings, and sensations that habitually orbit and support the old sense and feeling of self. And because of the challenge to one's identity, it also challenges not only the meaning but also the feeling of effort. For both the meaning and the feeling of effort, of struggle, are an essential part of what it means, and how it feels, to be a self, to think and feel 'I.'

The Struggle With Effort

Finally, then, the struggle is with the meaning and feeling of struggle itself, the meaning and feeling of effort. Once the challenge to one's feeling of self or identity is engaged, the struggle to find the meaning and feeling of effort must also be engaged. For the two – one's feeling of self and one's feeling of effort – are one and the same feeling.

The challenge presented to one's usual feeling of self is, in practical terms, a challenge to one's feeling of agency, to one's feeling of being an agent of change, whether of outer or inner conditions. This feeling must be embraced and encompassed by another feeling, a more authentic feeling, a feeling of Being. The usual feeling of agency must be lovingly attended as one would attend a dear child, with understanding and compassion. The very notion of agency must change.

The Struggle For Authentic Agency

Authentic agency is a movement of an active attention, anterior to all movement usually considered the acts of an agent. As one struggles to find the meaning and feeling of effort, one also struggles to discover a feeling of authentic agency.

Once again, an old feeling of agency finds itself challenged by a new, growing feeling of agency. A struggle ensues to find a new agent of change. Whereas before the "agent" was thought to be found sourced in this or that desire for this or that change, now the search is for a change agent that transcends and yet includes the entire level of conditioning, all the conflicting desires and the thoughts and tensions that serve them. The new agent of change is the new feeling of Self.

The New Agent's Struggle

The terms and conditions of struggle, then, are to be surrendered into the care of the new agent of change, the new and authentic Identity. Here we discover the meaning of submission to a higher purpose, a higher will.

Just as the authentic Self is an unknown agent of change, entirely other to the mistaken self, so authentic struggle or effort is an unknown force, entirely other to one's mistaken sense and feeling, one's initial understanding, of effort. The surrender of one's inauthentic feeling into the comprehensive embrace of authentic feeling constitutes the needed sacrifice of one's heedless sense of selfhood and agency.

By surveying several spiritual traditions in subsequent chapters, we will be able to find example after example of this process of surrender, the needed sacrifice of self before the wisdom of the nondual Agent.

CHAPTER TWO

TIBETAN BUDDHISM

The Buddhist Way

The Buddhist way was initiated by Gautama Buddha, an historical teacher of wisdom whose life, like the lives of so many such teachers, is shrouded in legend. He taught in the 6th century BCE, and is reputed to have lived to age 80.

The substance of his original teaching orbits what has been come to be known as the four noble truths: the fact of suffering, the cause of suffering, the way of liberation from suffering, and the eight practical steps leading to liberation. The Buddha was born into favorable circumstances; he was a prince, and he was shielded from the more baneful facts of life by his overprotective father. Once he discovered these facts, namely the facts of sickness, old age, and death, Gautama renounced his privilege and wandered as an ascetic, practicing severe physical and mental disciplines; consequently, after some time he began to approach total somatic enervation, thinking thereby to weaken the hold of attachment or desire, those features of clinging to varied objects of desire that were universally thought to cause suffering.

The Middle Way

Legend has it that one day Gautama, sitting in meditation, heard a passing boat in which was a maiden playing a stringed instrument. Suddenly he realized extreme ascetic practice was not the way to attain liberation. If the string is too tight, the sound will be distorted, he thought, and if it is too loose, the musician cannot play the instrument. The string must be just right, midway between too loose and too tight. Similarly, one cannot be too strict with oneself, for in so doing one will not attain liberation before one completely enervates the body-mind, and one cannot be too lax with oneself, for in so doing one will not be able to challenge one's usual sense and feeling of self, nor one's usual approach to desire or attachment.

Armed with this insight, Gautama decided to sit under the Bo tree until he attained enlightenment, which, legend has it, he eventually did. Thus he became the Buddha, the Awakened One. Subsequent to his awakening he began to teach the middle way to disciples, forming a monastic order of monks while also making provision for followers who remained active in ordinary life.

Buddhist Developments

It is well beyond the scope of this chapter to attempt a full accounting of later developments in the way of Buddhism; thus, we will consider only one such development, Tibetan Buddhism. Western readers are most familiar with such developments as Zen Buddhism in Japan, but in selecting Tibetan Buddhism we can also examine how the search for an understanding of effort is conducted in earlier forms of Buddhism as well.

Vajrayana Buddhism

According to the Dalai Lama, Tibetan Buddhism is the most complete form of Buddhism, for it includes earlier forms within its fold: Hinayana and Mahayana as well as Vajrayana.

There were originally eighteen schools of Hinayana Buddhism, the best known of which, at least in the West, is Theravada. Hinayana is known as the "lesser vehicle," and in its written form comprises all the earliest sutras or scriptures of the Buddha's discourses; in Tibet it is called the first turning of the wheel, that is, the first teachings, intended primarily for the earliest monastic community.

These earliest teachings are known as the path of renunciation; monks renounced the world, meaning ordinary life as it was then known in India: family, occupations, social life, all for the purpose of attaining enlightenment. The focus is on individual redemption or salvation, specifically liberation from ordinary desires or attachments and from one's ordinary identity.

The Mahayana form of Buddhism, known as the "greater vehicle," comprises what are held to be later discourses of the Buddha, known as the second turning of the wheel, and in written form comprised of later sutras, the best known being the Heart Sutra. Two substantial additions were made to the earlier teachings: first, the notion of emptiness, second, the idea of the bodhisattva.

The most remarkable expositor of this later development was Nagarjuna, who first taught the nondual doctrine in the East, and who further explicated the notion of a middle way. He created a logic that undermined all attempts to maintain a consistent conceptual notion of opposites, showing that each pole of a pair of opposites requires the other, that they cannot be conceptualized alone. He further taught that the idea of emptiness, or *shunyata*, can be approached by a thorough examination of the conceptual mind.

The idea of emptiness is that all phenomena, including our usual feeling of self, are empty of substance, are not substantial; objects as conventionally conceived are without substance; they do not exist as we conceive them to exist. They appear, but are appearances only with no real existence. Yet they are also not completely unreal, like imaginary objects: they are real appearances, manifesting out of, and returning to, emptiness. Reality, then, is empty of conventional conception, beyond concepts, and, therefore, beyond ego, our usual sense of self.

The Bodhisattva

The introduction of the bodhisattva ideal was revolutionary, for it put the liberation of others ahead of one's own liberation. The bodhisattva is that individual who, for the sake of others, postpones his own liberation, choosing instead to be reborn again and again until all other beings are liberated. The ideal of the Arhat, the Hinayana aspirant who attains liberation, is replaced by the Mahayana ideal of the bodhisattva.

The focus of interest, then, shifts from one's own redemption to the redemption of others. It is not that one's own liberation is deemed no longer important or essential; rather, it is that one's own liberation is incomplete, or more exactly not possible, so long as any being is unredeemed, trapped on the wheel of *samsara*, the world of attachment and desire, the world of suffering.

The Tantric Revolution

Still later in the development of Buddhism, around the 8th century CE, tantric ideas and methods were introduced not only into Buddhism but also the many forms of Hinduism. And it is these tantric ideas and methods that most distinguish Tibetan or Vajrayana Buddhism from the earlier Hinayana and Mahayana forms.

Tantric ideas and methods are intended to speed up one's progress toward liberation, analogous to what the 20th century teacher Gurdjieff called "hurry up yoga." Tantric teachings comprise what Tibetans call the third turning of the wheel of liberation, and the tantric scriptures are held to be the deliverances of the Buddha in his subtle bodily form, long after he had ceased to teach in his physical form.

Guru Yoga

Common to all the tantric schools of Tibet is the practice of guru yoga. Once again this chapter cannot trace developments in all these schools; hence, we will choose one school to examine: the oldest, the Nyingma school.

Devotion to a guru or spiritual teacher cuts across all authentic ways or paths to liberation, not only in Tibet but also the entirety of south central and southeast Asia, including parts of Asia Minor and the islands of Japan. The practice of guru yoga is the one constant throughout the varied spiritual traditions of Asia; these ways differ from one another in many respects while sharing a reverence for the guru. The reasons for this devotional attitude are many, but one reason has to do with the skillful transition from an ordinary idea of effort to an enlightened idea of effort, congruent with an overall liberated state of being.

Effort In Beginning Stages Of Practice

In beginning phases of Tibetan Buddhism, aspirants are advised to listen to a guru's discourses and sit in meditation. One begins with practicing *shamatha*, or "calm abiding," in one's sitting or meditation. Here the effort is to concentrate on a single object, which could be the light of a candle, an icon of a deity, or, as mentioned in the previous chapter, the breath. Usually the instruction is to concentrate on the breath.

We have already observed the difficulties involved in such a practice: one typically begins by following the breath, only to find that one's attention has wandered from the breath and is instead following a train of thought. Upon discovering a wandering attention, the effort is to gently bring the attention back to the breath. Also normal are the judgments regarding one's inability to remain with the breathing cycle. These are also considered distractions from the breath, so they must be treated as any other thought; one must immediately return to the breath without further thought about a given judgment.

The aim of the practice of calm abiding is to strengthen the attention and introduce the aspirant to the stillness and silence that forms the constant background to the usually noisy foreground of our thoughts and emotions. Both are very important, indeed essential, acquisitions to the individual, for they make possible entry into the deeper strata of the Vajrayana way or path. What interests us here most, however, is not the possible attainments but the sort of effort needed to make such attainments possible.

Even at this initial stage one can begin to taste a different sort of effort than that inculcated by family and society. Rather than a tense, muscular effort one is instructed to relax to the degree possible and be gentle and easy in one's redirecting of one's attention back to the breath, as well as the breathing itself, which should remain natural and unforced. The challenge for the aspirant is to follow these instructions, for they run counter to one's conditioning, to all one has learned about effort, about "trying."

Effort In Vipassana Meditation

After sufficient experience has been gained in calm abiding, and the aspirant has attained some ability to concentrate one's attention, one is instructed to sit or meditate upon whatever arises in one's awareness: a thought, emotion, somatic sensation, environmental sounds, smells, or sights, the latter, sights, depending upon whether one's eyes are open or closed. In Tibetan Buddhism, one's eyes are usually open in an unfixed gaze, allowing whatever sights to enter one's field of vision. This sort of meditation is called *vipassana.*

The effort here is to attend in an easy and relaxed manner whatever enters one's awareness; it requires a measure of concentration, already attained in the practice of calm abiding, because, again, the attention will wander away from the practice. One can easily misunderstand the instruction, especially as one begins to undertake the practice. Remaining with *what is*, with an active attention, is difficult. One begins by attending thoughts, for example, but ends by discovering that one has become lost in a train of associative thought, so much so that the other phenomena of awareness – the outer stimuli, for example – have also not been noticed or attended. There may have been emotional reactions to the associative thought process that have also gone unnoticed.

The effort, then, as it was in calm abiding, is to return one's attention to *all* contents of consciousness, including any reactions or judgments. The power of attending or concentrating developed in calm abiding will serve to make this effort more possible with less distraction. The difference is that rather than concentrating upon only one object of awareness, like the breath, one concentrates upon whatever happens to arise, or appear, in one's stream of consciousness. If the breath happens to appear, it is attended, if not, it isn't; the aspirant makes no attempt to make it appear, or make it disappear. The same holds true for any possible object of awareness: no phenomenon, whether a thought, feeling, or environmental, is made to enter awareness and, if it does, it is not made to leave. All are attended with an active attention developed previously in calm abiding.

Tantric Effort

Our task is to examine the meaning of effort in Tantric Buddhism without getting lost in the complexity of the differing stages even in only one school, the Nyingma. The bibliography at the end of this book will help orient any reader who wishes to explore this complexity. Consequently we will look at only one example of effort out of many that could be cited.

Having come some way by training the attention, a given aspirant, working with a guru, is instructed to visualize the mandala of a deity, perhaps a bodhisattva, and may or may not visualize the form of his own guru in place of the deity at the mandala's center. The visualization is often in front of one, but may also be above one's head.

After some training in this sort of visualization, another, more advanced set of instructions are given, by which the aspirant is told to visualize an inner mandala, that is, the subtle pathways within the body through which transformative energy flows, the *nadis* and also the *chakras*. Eventually, after considerable practice, the actual energy and its real inner channels and vortexes can be felt; at that point the visualization can be dropped and one is then instructed to attend the real flow of *prana*, *Shakti*, or life-force, having no need to imagine such a flow any longer.

The effort required at both these stages is, of course, an effort of attention, but in the first, imaginative stage one must call upon one's capacity to visualize. Some individuals are rather adept at visualization already, while others are not. So for some, perhaps most, aspirants the effort needed is rather considerable, though here again a tense, assertive, acquisitive effort, such as we learn in ordinary life, is counterproductive. But the fact remains that for most individuals the effort of attention required for visualization is more daunting than that needed either for calm abiding or *vipassana*.

The effort needed for the second stage, where one is asked to attend the actual flow of energy and notice the channels or *nadis* and the vortexes or *chakras*, is itself more subtle than that needed to visualize. Here the phenomenon that was previously only imagined has appeared as a real flow of life-force, and the effort is to allow this force to have its way, not to interfere or try to direct it in any way. The shift in effort, from an attempt to imagine this force to attend it, is considerable; although in some respects it resembles *vipassana* meditation, attending whatever arises, in other ways it is very different and much more demanding. It demands a degree of surrender unknown in any previous stages of practice. The effort, then, is primarily, and simultaneously, an active effort of attention and a surrender of effort altogether.

Dzogchen

Dzogchen, or Atiyoga, is considered the highest teaching in the Nyingma school of Tibetan Buddhism. It is called the "Great Perfection," and it is the culmination of the "pointing out" instructions which one's guru may, or may not, have given one much earlier.

The pointing out instructions are intended to introduce the aspirant to the nature of awareness or consciousness, to the natural state of being which is veiled by obscurations like our usual thoughts and feelings, but above all by our usual sense of identity. The guru is free to provide these instructions whenever he feels the devotee is ready for them, usually after some time with the guru. But the initial introduction is, after all, only an introduction; in order to benefit from it the aspirant must learn to abide in the natural state, first during sitting or meditation, later in ordinary life.

The idea of emptiness is used along with the idea of clarity, awareness. The natural state is not an experience but the empty, clear space within which experience arises and to which it returns. Presence is introduced as a recognition of the natural state, recognizing always already awareness as the natural state of being, as Being itself. Our true nature is the opening that neither comes nor goes; it is always already present, and the aspirant is instructed to practice recognizing it in the moment, whether on the meditation cushion or in the bustle of life. Experiences, by contrast, do come and go; they arise in the opening or lucid space that we are, and they subside in that space. We may experience calm abiding, or we may experience anxious cognition or feeling. Regardless of the experience, the open, empty spaciousness, the clear light of awareness, abides always and everywhere.

Effort In Atiyoga

The effort in this final stage of Vajrayana teaching is to attend Presence, recognize one's true nature, without being distracted by experience. One's efforts are intended to attain stability in recognizing the difference between awareness and experience.

Here we encounter a still more subtle effort, one that asks the aspirant not only to attend whatever arises as an experience but also recognize the always abiding natural state, Being itself. And these must be clearly distinguished: awareness itself, the empty opening in which experiences rise and fall, and the constantly changing experiences themselves, the changeless and the changed.

Winds Or Prana

The flow of life-force, what Tibetans call the "winds" and other traditions call *prana* or *Shakti*, plays an absolutely essential role in learning to recognize one's true nature, one's Buddha nature. For without the life-force, introduced in earlier phases of Tantric practice, an aspirant would have to rely on the ordinary mind to recognize the real, and the mind is a highly unreliable instrument.

Many well known Tibetan lamas, such as Trungpa, have spoken and written about the necessity of the life-force flowing through what Tibetans call the central channel of the body to recognizing Buddha nature. Awareness, or *rigpa*, is likened to a rider, and the higher energy, or *prana*, is likened to a horse: our true nature is recognized by the flow of the life-force through the central, vertical axis of the body. Without this indisputable flow of force, we would not be able to distinguish the awareness that accompanies it from the changing experiences of life.

When Tibetan gurus or lamas speak of being aware of awareness, or recognizing awareness, they do not refer to a disembodied mental phenomenon, as some might suspect, assume, or believe. Rather, they refer to an embodied flow of awareness, felt as higher energy, and also felt as a strong Presence. They emphasize that Buddha nature, Awareness itself, and the winds that carry it, always move together; one cannot be recognized without the other. Thus one can see the necessity of a previous training in tantric energetic practice.

The more complete account of effort in Atiyoga or Dzogchen, then, is a concentration upon an inner flow of life-force without being distracted by changing experience. Anyone who attempts to "do" this by their own efforts will soon discover it cannot be done. Yet there is something one must do, some "effort" needed.

Energetic Deposits

Assuming most aspirants will have practiced tantric methods for some time before entering the more demanding way of Atiyoga, they will have accumulated deposits of energy throughout the body, but particularly in the area that Zen calls the *hara*, the area around the navel. What cannot be done by the aspirant can be done by the spiritual force in, above, and around the physical body. This force, accumulated over the years, will itself call the aspirant to itself and, when called, the effort is to be faithful in one's surrender to it. Deposits of energy within the body correspond to the higher energy without and above; the energy above the head is invited to descend toward the center of gravity of the aspirant, the abdomen.

According to Anne Klein, an American lama in the Nyingma school, enlightenment is the flow of winds through the center of the body.

The Meaning Of Effort

In Vajrayana Buddhism the very meaning of effort changes as one moves from one stage of practice to another. At each new stage a more subtle effort is demanded, until at last the effort becomes an effortless waiting upon a higher force, and, when called, a surrender to it. Previous efforts of a training in attention were all necessary to be able finally to rest in one's true nature, completely relaxed, free of tension, still of emotion, silent of mind, surrendered into the life-current of Buddha, of Reality itself.

CHAPTER THREE

ADVAITA VEDANTA

Vedanta

Vedanta, a spiritual tradition originating in India, has had a major influence on Western spirituality ever since Vivekananda introduced it to the West in the late 19th century. The word Vedanta means the end of the Vedas, and its major scriptures are the Upanishads, those written dialogues or "seminars" between teacher and students that come at the end of the Vedic literature.

The Vedas describe the sacrificial system of ancient India; the most well known Veda, at least in the West, is the Rig-Veda. The Upanishads comprise a later development, reflecting a transition from outer forms of sacrifice to inner sacrifice of the conventional self-sense. This sacrifice is conducted through various forms of self-inquiry.

Advaita

The term Advaita means nondual; thus, Advaita Vedanta is a spiritual tradition that maintains that reality is "not-two," that reality is nondual, and that manifest reality is Consciousness or Awareness only. The appearance of independent entities and processes is an illusion – *if* they are seen as independent. If, on the other hand, they are understood as dependent, relative realities, dependent upon and made of Awareness, then they are real, but only in a relative, dependent sense.

The truths of Advaita are made available to all seekers, but in traditional Vedanta sufficient preparation is considered essential before one can expect even to begin to understand them. Thus the initial effort needed in this tradition is one of clearing away the many obstructions that prevent receiving the teaching. For this effort various yogas are needed.

Karma Yoga

For those who wish to remain in the world, who do not wish to renounce involvement with career and family, effort is applied in following the path of karma yoga. The basic idea of karma is that action undertaken with a mistaken sense of agency will have effects, most often effects that perpetuate the cycle of birth, suffering, and death. Karma yoga is intended to interrupt this cycle by performing actions without attachment to particular outcomes or results.

Even though the higher teaching is that through ignorance one believes one is a personal self which can undertake action, traditional Vedanta understands that beginners are not ready to receive this knowledge directly except through talks or discourses that are received by the intellect only. In order to prepare to receive Vedantic teaching more deeply, one must prepare the body-mind through *sadhana* or spiritual practice. Efforts must be made to disengage the attention from a mistaken sense and feeling of agency. For those involved in career and family, karma yoga is the suggested practice.

Bhakti Yoga

For those of a devotional bent, bhakti yoga is recommended. Here the effort is to turn one's attention away from normal preoccupation with one's mistaken sense and feeling of self to a wider or higher sense of self, usually a teacher, guru, or deity like Shiva. Coarse, egoistic feelings are refined in acts of devotion to the guru or deity.

Concentrated feelings of devotion weaken the usual self-love that helps to maintain a mistaken identity. Eventually the feeling is refined enough to begin to connect with a higher emotional source within oneself, previously unknown because of a lack of correspondence between egoistic feeling and higher feeling.

Jnana Yoga

Individuals who are more intellectual may find jnana or knowledge yoga more helpful in preparing the mind to receive authentic knowledge. This form of yoga relies heavily on discourses by a teacher or guru, and includes the method of self-inquiry.

This form of yoga also involves devotion, but it is not devotion directed toward a representative of reality, like a guru, but a devotion to the truth. In the beginning the effort is to listen attentively, have trust in the teaching, and begin to verify the teaching in one's inner laboratory through self-inquiry, questioning one's mistaken sense and feeling of self and agency.

Qualifications

The goal of the Vedantic quest is Self-realization, and the purpose of yoga and other methods of spiritual discipline is to qualify aspirants to be able to realize or recognize their authentic Identity. After a considerable period of time, several prerequisites for Self-realization have been determined to make that event more likely. What follows is not an exhaustive list but enough to give the reader some idea of what is involved, what qualities are produced by one's initial efforts on the Vedantic path.

One prerequisite is *viveka*, or discrimination, primarily the ability to discriminate the permanent from the temporal, the real Self from the ordinary sense and feeling of self. Another is *vairagya*, indifference or nonattachment. This quality is produced by a gradual withdrawal of attention from the apparent world of objects and concentrating one's attention upon the Self and the yogic disciplines like mantra meditation. Yet another, which will complete our partial list, is the one-pointed concentration of one's attention not only upon a chosen object in meditation but also upon the desire for liberation.

Initial Efforts

Beginning efforts on the Vedantic path, then, are intended to prepare one to recognize the Self, to attain Self-realization or enlightenment. In Advaita Vedanta, efforts include listening to the chanting of scriptures, intellectually assimilating often challenging ideas that run counter to one's ordinary intuition, and practicing faithfully the discipline of whatever form of yoga corresponds best to one's inclinations, whether intellectual, emotional, or physical.

To attempt to examine all these varied ways of approaching the same goal would be to exhaust ourselves unnecessarily; all that is needed is to select one line of effort in order to understand what is involved in them all. We will therefore confine our study to the line of self-inquiry, found primarily in the discipline of jnana yoga but also utilized in the other yogas as well.

Self-Inquiry

The effort of self-inquiry is a questioning of one's usual sense and feeling of identity; effort is required because this usual feeling is deeply rooted in the tissues of the body, and the teaching of Advaita is that this ordinary feeling obstructs our authentic feeling of Self.

Ramana Maharshi, Advaita's most renowned sage, recommended asking the question: Who am I? The effort needed to stay with this question is considerable, and is itself a training in concentration. Ramana taught that all thinking is rooted in what he called the I-thought, and if we examine our thoughts we find that they all orbit this notion and feeling of I. Whenever one of these countless thoughts appeared, Ramana advised returning to the question of identity: to whom does this thought occur? To me. Who am I?

One can readily see how much effort is required to stay with this question without wavering, and those first taking up the practice were no doubt unable to remain in the state of self-inquiry for long. With persistence, however, and with supplemental disciplines like meditation, the aspirant would develop enough attention to remain with self-inquiry for longer or, perhaps, simply more frequent periods of time.

What is the real nature of this self-inquiry? Is it to arrive at an intellectual piece of information? Obviously not, for in traditional Advaita training one is told straight away that one is choiceless, ordinary Awareness or Consciousness. No, the object of self-inquiry is to arrive at another kind of knowledge altogether, one that includes feeling and sensation, a form of knowledge that includes the entire body-mind complex. For the ordinary, mistaken self-sense is not confined to the intellect; it also involves the feeling and somatic structures.

Withdrawal Of Feeling

For that reason an essential part of the self-inquiry that Ramana taught was a withdrawal of the feeling of I from the content of thought, including specific objects of thought like desires, for these desires are fueled, indeed created, by Self-feeling, by the feeling of I. Concomitant with this effort was the instruction to search for this feeling just as one was turning one's attention inside, to be alert to the advent of the energy of the Self, the Shakti of Shiva.

Traditional Advaita does not highlight the activity of the higher energy, but Ramana taught that the higher Force or Energy was his authentic Identity manifested in the body. Anyone who turns inward in search of a more authentic feeling of I will discover this force. James Swartz, a contemporary teacher of Advaita Vedanta, refers to it as "just Shakti," which is emblematic of Advaita's inclination to downplay this important feature of inner development.

Shakti

In holding to the question of identity, Ramana suggests that eventually a given aspirant will make several essential discoveries, discoveries that will make possible subsequent inner developments leading to Self-realization. One such discovery is inner silence and stillness; another is Shakti.

Just as in the case of Tibetan Buddhism, the discovery of Shakti marks a definite transition in the journey of one's understanding of effort. For the continued reception of Shakti demands an altogether different sort of effort than that required in earlier phases of inner work. Before, the effort needed corresponded in many ways to our ordinary conditioning, our usual understanding of what it is to make effort. Not in all ways, of course, for even from the start one is told to relax even as one concentrates. After the discovery of Shakti, the effort to concentrate upon self-inquiry falls away naturally; with the advent of the higher Force one has discovered the authentic feeling of I, of Being, as well, and any further questioning of identity is counterproductive.

As with Tibetan Buddhism, the advent of Shakti is the birth of another identity, one that is the harbinger of another body, a higher organism that alone can lead to an authentic Self-realization, for only Shakti can dissolve the somatic tensions of the body-mind, where our mistaken sense of identity is held as if in a vise.

Another Kind Of Effort

The reception, assimilation, and transmission of higher energy demands another kind of effort, one that is counterintuitive to our conditioning, as indeed Vedantic teachings are counterintuitive. In meditation the effort amounts to little more than the initial movement of attention inside. In the activities of daily life, however, the effort is to return to an altogether different center of gravity.

Shakti first establishes this new center, and then points the way to it. It is this center, located in the area that Zen calls hara, that attracts higher energy from above and that becomes the wellspring for further ontological development. Confining the reception of Shakti to periods of sitting meditation is not sufficient for optimal inner growth of being; what is also needed is an ongoing placement of one's feeling of I in between lower and higher manifestations of Shiva. Standing under the higher, and over the lower, a new feeling of I, of identity, a new feeling of embodiment, is able to receive the creative work of Shakti amid the ordinary activities of life. It is this intermediate placement of the I that invites all subsequent discoveries and developments – including the Vedantic discovery of the real Self.

It is not that Advaita neglects the reception and assimilation of Shakti; it is just that this dimension of discovery and development is not given as central a place in its teaching as it is given in other spiritual traditions.

CHAPTER FOUR

KASHMIR SHAIVISM

The Tantric Tradition

Kashmir Shaivism is a tantric tradition that originated in northern India around the 8th century CE; its metaphysical teachings present, in mythological terms, the union of Shiva and Shakti as the primordial manifestations of ultimate reality. Shiva is the principle of pure awareness, while Shakti is the principle of creative energy.

In many respects the tantric tradition of Kashmir Shaivism is similar to the tantric tradition of Vajrayana Buddhism, but the differences are marked enough to merit a separate treatment in examining the transitional meanings of effort across varied spiritual traditions.

Spanda

Another teaching of this tradition is that there is a fundamental creative vibration, called spanda, that is at the source of all manifestation on all levels, including the level of the human being, and that the purpose of an inner discipline or sadhana is to come into contact with, and so have an awareness of, that vibration.

Consequently even the idea of the void, or emptiness, that the traditions speak of as the source of creation, is seen by this tradition as a plenum of force, pulsing with this basic creative energy. In the human being, according to Kashmir Shaivism, this force is known as Shakti or kundalini.

Kundalini

Teachers of this tradition usually speak of kundalini only in its dormant state; when activated by inner work, it is referred to as prana or Shakti, and is felt as a circulation of energy, traveling through the channels or nadis, touching and opening the centers of energy, or chakras, of the subtle body.

Overall, the basic idea of engaging the varied stages of inner work is to release somatic tensions and allow this Shakti or basic energy of Being or the Self to flow, to become familiar with this flow, and to learn to identify it as one's authentic Identity.

Nonduality

Kashmir Shaivism is another nondual tradition. Reality, that is, is not-two – not even one, which implies also two or more. And for this teaching, reality is this energy, or rather the inseparable unity of Shiva and Shakti, Awareness and Energy, that Swami Chetanananda calls dynamic stillness.

Kashmir Shaivism sees this energy as being essential to the eventual understanding of reality itself, essential to Self-realization. In that regard it reveals itself as a tradition decisively influenced by the overarching tantric tradition that has had an impact on many inner ways of liberation that have emerged from India.

The method of this teaching, its way of assisting aspirants, divides into three parts: guru or teacher, individual meditation and reflection, and service to others. Each of the three is implicated in the different stages of inner work that each aspirant must pass through; we will examine these stages, as they help illustrate the growing understanding of effort in this tradition. These stages are called strategies.

The Strategy Of Individual Effort

A newcomer to this way of working enters the path adopting what is called the strategy of individual effort. At this initial stage the aspirant learns the mechanics, the rules of working alone, for example in solitary meditation, and the rules of working with a guru and the community or ashram that has gathered about the teacher. At the same time, a given beginner, from the outset, is introduced to a new way of working, a new way of making efforts, counter to the holding culture's conditioning.

At this stage the aspirant is introduced to breathing, to the chakras, to the flow of energy, and to the need to develop the attention required to attain a measure of experiential knowledge of these processes. A student is advised to withdraw at least two-thirds of his attention from outer concerns and concentrate on a developing inner life. This tradition characterizes all this as dissolving inner tensions and releasing a flow of creative energy.

The Strategy Of The Energy

Eventually the energy will reveal a new center of gravity, and with that revelation one enters a new stage, called the strategy of the energy. The creative energy that has been allowed to flow within becomes the focus of a new sense and feeling of identity: not the old feeling inculcated by the holding culture, but a new feeling of the Shakti of life itself, the life-force as felt in the body.

The teacher, once seen as a person with characteristic features and flaws, is now seen as an authentic guru, an embodiment of the life-force, and, as such, an energetic source of the teaching or tradition itself.

With this important shift in identity, one is led by the flow of energy within as it takes on a life of its own, connected to yet independent of the physical body. Old identifications begin to lose their hold in the blinding light of the life-force, in particular the identification with the body, but also, and equally significant, the finding of one's identity in thoughts and emotions. As the circulation of the life-force strengthens, these forms of identity weaken.

Because the focus of attention is an energy with its own life, the meaning of effort also shifts, from a kind of doing in the earlier stage to a kind of knowing, an effort to sustain a recognition of the significance of this Shakti. It is a kind of awareness that is there whenever either one recognizes it or it recognizes one. Either way, it is one's new identity: "it" is I.

This tradition emphasizes the identity between Shiva and Shakti, between Awareness and Energy. As highlighted above, the reception and recognition of higher energy not only helps to weaken old identifications but it also helps to move one away from a psychological orientation toward an energetic orientation. And this transition to an interest in energy in turn leads to a growing interest in awareness, in awareness as the Self.

The Strategy Of The Self

In the strategy of individual effort, the focus is on doing; in the strategy of the energy, the focus is on knowing; in the strategy of the Self, the focus is on awareness, that is, the Self.

To focus on the Self is to train attention on awareness itself; it is an awareness of awareness. The changing experiences we have are seen to be manifestations of, energetic expressions of, changeless awareness. All experience is an expression of Awareness, an expression of the Self, whether inside or outside the conventional body-mind identity.

In earlier stages the aspirant had to discriminate between his true Identity and partial identities; now the individual turns to life understanding that all things, all events, all processes, are the Self, that every experience is an experience of the Self, that he is one with the All, with Awareness.

Higher energy still reveals a higher level of awareness that we need if we are to continue to grow, to develop, but one can now understand that the Self is recognized in all experience, even in the absence of a felt higher Being-energy. In some traditions the attempt is made to move from ordinary experience directly into seeing all as one; in Kashmir Shaivism, however, one must pass through the strategy of the energy before one can learn to recognize the Self in all and everything.

In this most subtle stage of work the effort becomes a simple recognition of the Self as the source and substance of all experience, high, low, and middling. Whenever the mind remembers, the energy is called or, rather, noticed; when the energy is felt, the mind remembers. One supports the other. The simple recognition of Awareness, however it occurs, is all the effort that is needed.

CHAPTER FIVE

TAOISM

The Watercourse Way

Taoism, the "watercourse way," is said to have been born in ancient China with Lao Tzu and his *Tao Te Ching*, often translated into English as *The Way and Its Power*. Lao Tzu is a legendary figure, said to have flourished in the 6th century BCE; he was a librarian who, when leaving China in his later years, wrote this short testament to his life and work.

Other translations of this short book leave the word *Tao* untranslated, partly because the book itself says that the Tao that can be spoken or written is not the real Tao: it is a reality beyond the ordinary mind. Nevertheless, in trying to speak or write about it, the Tao may be said to be a "way" in three senses: first, the way of reality itself; second, the way of nature or the natural world; and third, the way of the human being. It is called the watercourse way because of all natural phenomena – the Tao in its second meaning – water is seen as most akin to the first meaning, reality itself, and also most akin to the completed human being.

Water is "humble," it seeks the low places; it is "accommodating," it flows effortlessly around barriers and obstacles; it is life-giving, refreshing all living things; and it is powerful, in its surging carrying all before it, carving out canyons and wearing away seashores. These features of water, particularly the action in inaction, the power of yielding, become for Taoists emblematic of the perfected human being.

Two Taoisms

Two types of Taoist thinking and acting are of interest in our study: the first is intellectual or philosophical Taoism; the second is Taoist yoga. Intellectual Taoism is concerned with *wu wei*, translated as "letting be." Here the Taoist is interested in discovering what power or *te* is already available, and working effectively with that in order to align oneself with the Tao of the natural world and reality itself. Taoist yoga is an approach that seeks not only to discover power but also to augment it, to become better able to align oneself with the Tao of nature and reality. In higher stages both discovery and development are found to be in reciprocal relation with each other; at the beginning, however, the two types of Taoism focus on different approaches.

Taoist Yoga

For purposes of our study, we will confine ourselves to examining the second form of Taoism, Taoist yoga. Like other traditions that practice yoga, Taoists are interested in the life-force, the energy, that comprises and pervades the natural world and reality itself. Indian yogic traditions call it *prana*; Chinese yogic traditions call it *ch'i*.

Two traditions comprise Taoist yoga: the fire tradition and the water tradition. The fire tradition came about through interaction with Tibetan yoga and its way of discovering the life-force: visualization or imagination. As in Tibetan Buddhism, the subtle inner environment is visualized in as much detail as possible, including the energy centers called chakras and the nadis or channels through which the energy flows. The effort of visualization is sustained until one actually discovers the inner, energetic flow of force.

The water tradition comports better with Taoist thought, particularly in Taoist literature. Rather than visualize the subtle centers and channels within the body, the effort is to sense or feel what is available for immediate sensation and feeling. It may be that for some time one can only sense and feel the body itself, but over time one is encouraged by elders to sense and feel the inner space within the body, until one discovers a growing life inside, including subtle energetic centers and movement.

Taoist Alchemy

Closely allied to yoga is alchemy, and in China both were practiced as ways to augment *te*, the force or power of life. Like the medieval alchemists of Europe, efforts were made to discover substances that would enhance and even extend life indefinitely. For many alchemists, these efforts were abandoned in favor of an inward, alchemical transformation of substances within, the physical body acting as the athanor or oven.

To help invite the reception and assimilation of *ch'i*, alchemists and yogis alike developed movement technologies, the best known in the West being *t'ai-chi chuan*. In addition to inviting the life-force, these movements were intended to help remove the obstructions, usually somatic tensions and thoughts, that prevent the reception of higher energy. The movements are usually performed slowly, and as students progress teachers admonish them to relax more and more as they move.

The practice of seated meditation is of course included, as it is in all spiritual traditions. Taoist meditation is intended, again, to remove obstructions such as tensions and discover the life-force, developing the inner life along the way. Eventually the aspirant learns to balance the inner and outer life in a harmonious relationship.

Awareness Itself

Taoist elders teach that without the body it is not possible to discover pure awareness, awareness without content. Awareness they liken to a mirror; the contents of awareness they liken to red dust. Like somatic tensions, the "red dust" of awareness, which is comprised primarily of thoughts, make it difficult to discover the mirror-like quality of awareness.

Enter the life-force. For it is the entry, the discovery, of the life-force that makes possible the discovery of awareness itself. Taoists teach that the discovery of pure awareness depends upon the central nervous system and its ability to receive the formless energy of awareness along the central axis of the body.

Creating A Soul

Taoist teaching is not focused primarily upon enlightenment; rather, its focus is upon an intermediate attainment: the creation of a *ling*, or soul, a kind of second body or vehicle in between the ordinary sense of self and the real Self, between lower and higher worlds, between the two great movements of energy, the movement away from the Source and the movement of return to the Source.

Thus the teaching of *wu-wei* or non-doing can be seriously misunderstood if it is taken as a kind of passive "letting be" involving no effort, *sahdana*, or spiritual discipline. Although the effort involved, even in initial stages, is counter to effort as taught in the outer world, it still demands an active attention to the creation of a new being within oneself, the creation of a new ability to live in between the two worlds or forces of the cosmos without being consumed by either.

This creation of a "soul" is attained through the reception of higher energy and its gradual accumulation of energetic deposits within the body. Over time, these deposits form an indestructible force.

Immortality

Traditional Chinese culture has always been interested in extending life indefinitely, and as previously mentioned Chinese alchemists attempted to discover and formulate physical elixirs that would bring immortality to the physical body.

Alchemy in its authentic form, however, turned from this more primitive interest to an interest in attaining immortality through the creation of a soul or second body using the first or physical body as an athanor, an oven, in which inner substances already contained within the first body would be mixed with higher energies or substances received and, using the fire or heat of inner work, produce an intermediate, energetic form or body that will survive the death of the physical form. For this creation effort of a subtle sort is needed.

Initial Effort

As in all authentic spiritual traditions, the initial effort in Taoist yoga is to discover and nurture the still mind, to discover the "great stillness."

This discovery is best accomplished in seated meditation, although it can also be discovered, more rarely, in moving meditation. And, as in other traditions, the effort involved is in learning to concentrate attention upon a single focus, for example the breath.

Dissolving

Once one has attained a still mind, the process of dissolving obstructions to receiving higher energy can begin. Dissolving involves scanning the body for blockages and letting them go using attention; this practice can be performed seated, standing still, or moving, movement usually performed in slow motion.

The practice of dissolving demands guidance from an elder, for it can release traumas and high-voltage emotional energies that need to be addressed and, perhaps for a time, left alone. The practice of dissolving emotional blockages to the passage of higher energy involves a shift in interest from the psychological, with its judgments and thoughts about the emotion, to the energetic, sensing and feeling the energy of the emotion and letting the thoughts about the emotion be without getting caught up in them.

Here, in this practice of dissolving, we have not only a good example of the sort of effort required but also of a combination of "letting be" and active inner work. The active part of the effort is in attending the emotional energy; the passive or "letting be" part is in allowing thoughts to arise and fall without identifying with them.

Receiving Higher Energy

Once obstacles or blockages are sufficiently dissolved, the aspirant is poised to make the most momentous discovery: the discovery of an energy descending from above the head along the vertical axis of the body, the reception of a higher substance that can begin the formation of a soul, a second body.

The water method of Taoist yoga, unlike the fire method characteristic of Tibetan yoga, begins with discovering the current sensations and feelings in the body as one directs attention within. No attempt is made to visualize either the centers of energy or the channels along which energy travels. Taking one's attention within the body, the yogin simply senses and feels whatever is there to sense and feel.

A great deal of this inner work will have already been accomplished during the dissolving stage; however, the effort is no longer to dissolve blockages but just to discover the different energies currently inhabiting the body that has by and large been cleared of obstacles. The effort here is a gentle allowing of whatever is inside to appear in awareness.

The work of allowing, this most disciplined yet subtle of efforts, will not only invite the discovery of higher energy but will also extend into the ongoing development of a *ling*, a "soul" or second body. Once the higher energy begins to flow, it is most important not to direct it willfully: this energy is intelligent, and knows not only its way but also what needs to be accomplished in a particular athanor. And it will also remove any residual obstacles to its free movement.

CONTEMPLATIVE CHRISTIANITY

Esoteric Christianity

Our study of contemplative Christianity will not attempt to describe or discuss in any detail the exoteric or doctrinal teachings that have issued in so many theological divisions within the Christian tradition. We will instead study contemplative Christianity from the perspective of the two major churches: the Roman Catholic church in the West, and the Orthodox church in the East. These two traditions are esoteric in two senses: first, they penetrate inward to the heart and soul of the human being, and second, they are relatively inaccessible in that a given individual must seek them out; they are not taught to conventional church goers, nor are they sought out by nominal Christian believers.

Contemplative Prayer

In the West, the Catholic church, over the centuries and in its monastic enclaves, has developed what has come to be known as contemplative prayer, or *lectio divina*. It is a process of praying that involves hearing a passage of holy writ or scripture, meditating upon it, then entering a state of inward quiet called contemplation, wherein one opens to the always already Presence of God, a process that Abbot Thomas Keating calls receiving.

Effort is required first of all simply to listen to the sacred words that are being read; they are usually read aloud in communities or schools of aspirants that the Catholic church calls "religious." This initial, relatively exoteric effort runs counter to our conditioning; by and large we are not taught how to listen attentively; we may begin listening well, but all too soon we drift away from the reading as our thoughts about more personal matters take us away. The effort, then, is to attend the reading so that we may begin to meditate, or reflect, on it.

The effort involved in meditation or reflection is very near to what we mean by pondering: having heard the selected reading, we make a determined effort to keep its central ideas or themes before our hearts and minds, returning again and again to them throughout the day, whether we are active in our roles in life or sitting quietly in the privacy of our "prayer closet."

To enter into contemplation proper is to enter into the most subtle effort of all in the Western Christian tradition. Before examining that effort, however, it would be helpful to rehearse briefly how an organization like Keating's Contemplative Outreach got started.

Centering Prayer

Centering prayer is a method of approaching contemplative prayer or contemplation developed in the late 20th century by monastics like Thomas Keating and Basil Pennington. They believed that those Christians not called to the monastic life should be able to take advantage of the full benefits of Christian spirituality, as Vatican II had directed.

An outreach program was needed because over a period of several centuries the notion of contemplation, of contemplative Christianity, was lost to all except for a few contemplative monastic orders such as the Cistercians. Keating and his colleagues, taking a cue from the mantra spirituality of the East, created a method of prayer that would help those unfamiliar with contemplative prayer to approach contemplation more readily.

Interested Christians would be invited to an initial, informal meeting where one or more experienced practitioners would introduce them to the method; these experienced individuals were as often as not lay people who had received training directly from Keating or his appointed representatives. After a brief introduction, beginners are asked to select a "sacred word," a word that held no excessively personal meaning for the individual, but one that would bring them back to inner stillness.

The method of returning to a sacred word is both like and unlike mantra meditation. In mantra meditation, a word or phrase, usually chosen by the guru, is given to help quiet the mind; without it, the beginning meditator in particular falls prey to the noisy head brain, where thoughts careen off one another in associations that prevent coming to a calm, still mind. The mantra is to be repeated continually, with each breath; in this way other thoughts are prevented from arising and, if they do in spite of the mantric repetition, they are not followed in associative chains.

The returning to a sacred word in centering prayer is unlike mantra meditation in two ways: first, no guru chooses the word; the aspirant chooses it; and second, the word is not to be repeated continually; it is returned to whenever the individual sees that the mind has strayed from silence. To be sure, for the beginner the word may need to be repeated almost continually, but later, as the individual tastes inner stillness, it will be utilized less and less as one learns to rest in Presence.

This method is also like mantra meditation in that it is also intended to help quiet the mind so that the aspirant may experience the inner quiet and stillness that is always available but veiled by egoistic thoughts.

Consent

Centering prayer, intended to help individuals attain contemplation, also introduces aspirants to the most subtle effort in Christian prayer: consent. For the Christian contemplative there are two types of will: egoistic will, the sort of effort about which we and our holding culture are most familiar, and a kind of receiving, what Keating calls consent.

Make no mistake, however, receiving, consenting to God's Presence, is not easy; it is very difficult. That is why those with no experience in a sheltered, monastic enclave need a catalyst like centering prayer, a way to approach this difficulty. According to Keating, "receiving is one of the most difficult kinds of activity there is." He argues that any notion of "trying" has a diluting effect on the reception of God's grace or Presence. And it is precisely this idea of trying that so characterizes what the holding culture teaches in its educating us about the meaning of effort.

If one insists on retaining the notion of effort in spiritual practice, Keating would remind that one that it is "totally unlike any other kind of effort. It is simply an attitude of waiting for the Ultimate Mystery," a journey into the unknown.

The Philokalia

For anyone interested in Eastern Orthodox prayer and discipline, the *Philokalia* is an indispensable work to consult. In that work, a collection of writings by Orthodox hermits and anchorites, one will find essentially the same ideas and even methods found in Western monasticism, including the idea that, as one ascends in one's spiritual growth and development, effort becomes less and less "effortful" and more and more a matter of relaxed invitation or allowing – in effect, consenting to God's Presence.

Nepsis

In the Orthodox Christian tradition the notion of *nepsis*, attentiveness or watchfulness, is key in approaching both prayer and effort. Writers in the *Philokalia* insist that authentic prayer is impossible without watchfulness, and watchfulness does not develop without a proper preparation of the body.

A certain division of the attention is required. Our normal attentiveness is more akin to ordinary perception than it is to an authentic state of consciousness; our attention flows outward, away from the source of our being toward phenomenal reality, which can be a thought, emotion, or sensation as easily as it can be a visual or auditory object. Orthodox teaching is that one's attention must be divided: one part allowed to flow outward toward objects of attention; the other part flowing inward toward the Source, toward God's energies within the body.

Authentic Prayer

Authentic prayer, then, cannot be the prayer of one asleep to God's Presence; one has to be aware of that Presence by attending to the flow of higher energy within the body. Orthodox Christianity speaks of this requirement as a joining of mind and heart.

According to Bishop Kallistos Ware, the word translated as heart means the center of one's being, a center that is discovered through the effort of attending God's Presence in authentic, watchful prayer. The attention of the mind must join with the attention of the body and kept there. God's energies will make deposits in that center, deposits that eventually create an indestructible force, an inner power that makes possible genuine communion with God, with Being itself.

Guarding The Heart

Common to both Eastern and Western forms of contemplative Christianity is the idea of guarding the heart. The basic inspiration for this notion is found in the New Testament, the letter of St. Paul to the Philippians, where he discusses prayer in chapter four.

According to St. Paul, God promises only one blessing in response to prayer: the peace that passes understanding. Paul writes that the Christian should make his requests known to God in prayer, not to inform God about one's desires, but to establish a relationship with Him, to feel His Presence. God may, or may not, answer prayer by meeting one's requests, but whether He does or not, He does promise to bless one with peace, and it is this peace, again according to the scripture, that will guard the heart.

Peace

In all the traditions we have examined so far, initial efforts are always made to establish and maintain a quiet mind. Why does the mind, or heart, need to be guarded? From what does the heart or heart-mind need to be protected?

Contemplative Christianity might say that the heart-mind needs to be guarded against attacks by the "enemy," from temptations to sin or succumb to negative influences such as egoic desires or harmful thoughts. Authentic prayer is meant to protect one from succumbing to baneful psychic influences, and, like we have seen in other traditions, the practice of making effort in meditation or prayer is a preparation for receiving the peace of God.

Effort And Grace

What better place in our survey to discuss the relationship between effort and grace than when examining the Christian tradition, a tradition that so often alludes to grace and "works" in its teachings? Extreme doctrinal positions in Christianity tend to emphasize either grace alone or effort, works, as decisive in obtaining salvation. More moderate theologies strike a balance between the two.

In the context of our survey, and again avoiding doctrinal disputes, we can identify effort as essential in the reception of grace, yet it is an effort already tinged with grace in that the initial teachings that an aspirant receives already begin to orient the individual away from the culture's notion of effort toward a more refined, spiritual idea, an idea congruent with the further and ongoing reception of grace.

For grace will not yield, or respond, to ordinary efforts. What is called "storming the gates of heaven" will not work. Grace will only descend when ordinary efforts cease, when a given aspirant raises a flag of surrender, dies to all ambition, and submits in humility to the active force of God. This act of authentic free will is what Christianity, in concert with other spiritual traditions, calls receiving grace.

CHAPTER SEVEN

ESOTERIC JUDAISM

Exoteric Judaism

Exoteric Judaism, the tradition of teachings that inform the Jewish way of life, is not our concern, just as the doctrines of Christianity did not concern us in the previous chapter. Tracing the development of the exoteric Jewish way is quite beyond the scope of our study and interest.

At the same time, some attention must be given to the outer form of the tradition in order to trace the movement of a given practitioner from an outer orientation to a more inner or esoteric orientation to that individual's unique spiritual path.

The Teaching

Exoteric Judaism is a teaching which is sometimes wrongly conceived as a system of law that must be obeyed. That is not an accurate rendition of Torah, the revealed teaching to the Jewish people, intended to be a perpetual reminder of their relationship to the God of the Hebrew Bible.

Also mistaken is the Christian idea that the New Testament or covenant is the rule of love, while the so called Old Testament or covenant is the rule of law; the contrast is usually made to suggest the superiority of the former to the latter. The truth is that the covenant between the Hebrew God and the Jewish people is also one of love, as illustrated clearly in such scriptures as Hosea. The commandments given are not intended to be burdensome; rather, they are constant reminders of God's abiding Presence, and this becomes ever more evident as a given aspirant moves from an exoteric to an esoteric point of view.

Sanctification

Every part of Jewish life is sanctified – set apart – by the teaching and by the specific commandment that addresses that part of life. Effort in living the teaching begins here, in the attempt to keep the commandments.

The strictly exoteric view may seem to permit a rote, obligatory approach to life, but such is yet another misunderstanding of the spirit of the Jewish way of life. Depending on the approach, whether ultra-Orthodox/Hasidic, Orthodox, Conservative, Reform, or Reconstructionist, certain demands are made upon the individual who attempts to conform to that approach to the Jewish tradition. If such a one does make the attempt in a rote fashion, without heart or spirit, that individual is not actually keeping the command in the spirit in which it was given. It amounts to a subtle form of avoidance, going through the motions while actually attending something one considers more important. One's attention, one's heart, is elsewhere, and the tradition considers such empty form idolatry.

Kavanah

Although keeping the outer form of the commandments requires effort, it is a form of effort not unlike that prescribed by the holding culture, the effort to attain a goal in ordinary life, for example. The transition to a more subtle effort begins with the intentional practice of *kavanah*.

The practice of *kavanah* requires a certain ingathering of attention, a concentration of inner force, aimed at performing a given commandment for its own sake, without any regard for results or outcomes. Whatever the prescribed action, it is undertaken with all one's heart, all one's attention, aimed at remembering God as incarnated not only in the activity but also in one's Self.

This way of performing *mitzvot* is a definite step beyond an ordinary, exoteric way of acting, even if one is in a profound state of devotion. For in a state of devotion one can still be attached to outcomes, thinking that God's approval rests there. With *kavanah*, by contrast, one recognizes that fellowship with God abides during the act itself, regardless of result, and that the outcome of a given action is better left to God. Thus one's investment of energy is in the performance of the act, not in any anxiety about any result, such as pleasing God.

Hitbonenuth

An even further refinement in effort can be found in the Jewish practice of *hitbonenuth*. This approach to keeping the commandments specifically includes the Self in the activity. That is, rather than an exclusive concentration upon the act, one also includes an awareness of one's Self: not the socially conditioned self, the bogus identity, but the authentic Self, manifested as a dynamic or energetic stillness.

Biblical And Talmudic Influences

The Jewish mystical tradition is rooted in the Hebrew Bible and also in Talmudic commentaries. This tradition makes a connection between biblical prophecy and a mystical cleavage to God, a connection difficult to follow for an exoteric practitioner. For that reason many rabbinic scholars that contributed to the forming of the Talmud are suspicious of this connection and warn possible aspirants to holiness to avoid it.

The more exoteric view of the phenomenon of prophecy is that God selects a worthy individual, reveals to that person that a message needs to be delivered, and commissions him to proclaim it, usually to those in positions of authority and power. Such messages often reveal God's judgment about a given state of affairs, and with that judgment a call to repentance is also issued, along with an account of unsavory consequences should the recipient ignore God's demands.

A popular misunderstanding of this exoteric view of prophecy is that the prophet is primarily a soothsayer, giving predictions about what will occur in the future. In this regard the prophetic paradigm is Jonah: God tells Jonah to deliver a message of repentance to the people of Ninevah, along with the consequences if they fail to repent. Jonah disobeys God by assuming that Ninevah is doomed anyway, and does not reveal what God demands. After some delays, including the red herring bit about the big fish, Jonah does deliver the command and Ninevah does repent. Because of their repentance God does not impose any untoward consequences upon the people. Thus the central motif of the prophecy is the restoration of the people of Ninevah, not the dire prediction of what would happen if they failed to repent. Neither Jonah nor any other prophet is a soothsayer in the sense of predicting a certain outcome.

Esoteric Prophecy

A more esoteric understanding of the phenomenon of prophecy accepts the exoteric understanding while penetrating deeper into the heart-centered relationship between prophet and God. The Judaic esoteric tradition shies away from speaking about union with God and prefers the phrase cleavage to God. A prophet is one who has been singled out, chosen by God to enter into a closer, more ecstatic relationship with Him. In the Hebrew scriptures, for example, early prophets were often bands of ecstatic individuals filled with the *shekinah* glory or energy of God, such energy usually unchanneled, whereas the later prophets, more familiar to most of us, channeled their energies to specific audiences.

It is therefore likely that, particularly in earlier eras, the prophetic phenomenon included both channeled and unchanneled varieties, some prophets hearing and responding to a clear message to be given to a specific audience, while others were filled with the divine energy, ecstatic in their pronouncements without feeling a call to deliver a specific message to a given audience. Later examples of this latter phenomenon abound, as in the Hasidic ecstatics of 18th century Eastern Europe.

Hasidism

The scholars who composed and compiled the Talmud believed that cleavage to God was best attained by a one-pointed devotion to the teaching first given by God to Moses, to a disciplined study of this teaching in community with others equally devoted.

This practice embodies a notion of effort that is sufficiently different from any holding culture to warrant attention. For the objective of such study was not something attainable in the egoic sense; it was its own reward, and cleavage to God was not something awaiting a future development such as mastery of Talmudic studies; rather, such cleavage was available in the moment of devotion to study, an act of worship in itself. One could also practice both *kavanah* and *hitbonenuth* as well.

Yet human nature being forgetful, and familial-societal conditioning being so strong, Talmudic studies tended toward the reinforcement of ego and the instituting of a kind of academic mentality. In addition, only a certain type of gifted individual was well suited for this way, leaving others in the Jewish community to tend to more ordinary affairs of life. Such individuals had to discover other ways to cleave to God, and out of this collective wish the Hasidic movement was born.

The Baal Shem Tov, the master of the good name, or Besht, initiated a more ecstatic way of cleaving to God, not just through study or through the *mitzvot*, but through music, dance, song, and spontaneous outbursts of what was often labeled prophecy. Over time communities of Hasidim formed around such charismatic figures, known as Rebbes, figures who appeared to cleave to God more readily or consistently, and whose presence helped others in their wish to attain such cleavage.

Effort, then, could be approached in two ways: the first, and more common, was and is to treat the Rebbe as an intermediary between God and the more usual individual in the community; the second, far less common and far more demanding, was and is to practice *kavanah* and *hitbonenuth* while participating in the song, dance, and ecstatic utterances of the Rebbe and his devotees.

The Rebbe's Example

The Rebbe, having attained cleavage to God, sets an example that few can follow. For that reason the majority of Hasids draw inspiration from him and are devoted to the Rebbe as God's chosen. Hasidism, then, has become an established way of being conventionally religious, no different in essence than the Orthodox, Conservative, or Reform ways of being Jewish. Whenever a spiritual movement attracts many followers, and those have children who are brought up to be followers, the notion of a highly subtle effort remains well beyond the reach of most.

Here as elsewhere, the effort needed is a complete divestment of the usual notion of identity and agency, submitting to the will of God in a way quite foreign and therefore quite remote and unlikely for the vast majority of religionists. Yet there remains a call set by the example of the Rebbe, a call for authentic identity and agency delivered as a prophetic challenge to the remnant.

The Remnant

The notion of a remnant, of a few individuals who remain faithful to God in the midst of an idolatrous and rebellious majority, has played an important and recurrent role in Jewish history and its religious and spiritual thought. But the demands placed upon those who wish to be a part of the remnant are severe, and few can be expected even to wish to accept the challenge.

In the Jewish esoteric tradition, the challenge is not simply to keep the *mitzvot* or commandments, those ritualistic behaviors that sanctify the profane, nor is it simply to gather with devotion about a charismatic figure. Rather, it is to seek an inward relationship with divine energy, and for that room must be provided within the heart, mind, and somatic structure, room to receive the descent of the *shekinah* glory of God.

The difficulty, the challenge, is in making room within. For it demands the utter surrender of the mind's hegemony as well as the profound release of somatic tension; it demands an effort unlike any taught either by the holding culture or the exoteric religious establishment; it demands a welcoming spirit that issues in no less than an authentic homecoming.

And few there be that find it.

CHAPTER EIGHT

SUFISM

Esoteric Islam

Islam is considered by its adherents to be God's final revelation to man; the word itself means submission, and a Muslim is one who has submitted himself to God's will as delivered in the Koran.

Whenever a religious tradition becomes dominant and its adherents possess much political power and wealth, the sacred elements tend to fall into neglect while profane elements command more attention. The inner *jihad* or struggle, which Muhammed singled out as of primary importance, also tends to suffer neglect as power-possessing individuals enjoy the fruits of conquest and imperious rule.

The origin of the name Sufi is debated by scholars, but it likely originated from the term *suf*, which means wool, partly because the earliest Sufis wore rough wool garments in protest of the fine, luxuriant linen worn by Islamic rulers. To the Muslim mystic or esoteric, the fine clothing symbolized spiritual decadence, while his own simple garment symbolized authentic submission.

Submission

The esoteric meaning of Islam is most profound, for it cuts across all authentic spiritual traditions; the notion of submission is at the core of every inner way or path to freedom. Without submission, no inner or ontological development is possible; with it, a given aspirant can receive the *barakah* or blessing from above.

The effort of submission for the exoteric Muslim is in submitting to the commands of God as revealed in the Koran. Here as elsewhere, it is not possible to survey all the rites and practices of this tradition, so we will select the instruction to pray five times daily. The call to prayer, heard five times daily, is a reminder not only of the prayer time but also, and more centrally, a reminder of God's majesty and uniqueness: God is great, there is no god but God, Muhammed is His prophet, come to prayer, remembering the greatness of God.

The most obvious exoteric effort is simply to come to prayer as called five times daily. The repeated prostrations of this rite symbolize submission to God. Such an act would seem to invite a deep intention, a more esoteric invocation of one or more of the names of God as a way of remembering God and forgetting self. Yet most leaders of exoteric Islam are suspicious of the deliberate attempt to practice other rites intended to remember God, rites of the dervishes of the Sufi orders: music, dance, song, invoking the names of God, *zikhr*.

Forgiveness For Separate Existence

The exoteric Islamic practice of asking for divine pardon for sin or transgressions is common to all Muslims; the more inner or esoteric practice of seeking forgiveness for one's existence is confined to Sufi orders.

It is not forgiveness for an act that is sought, but forgiveness for a state of being, a state that separates the dervish from the only Reality, symbolized by God. This state of separation is very like the Christian notion of original sin, which is not a sin committed but a state of separation into which one is cast simply by being born into a fallen world. It has nothing to do with anything one has done or failed to do, but has to do with having been tricked into a mistaken sense of identity, one that ignores the actual Condition of existence or Being itself. And it is this mistaken sense of self for which the Sufi asks forgiveness, for which he feels a sense of remorse and from which he seeks to be delivered with God's help.

There Is Nothing But God

The exoteric Muslim's call to prayer proclaims that there is no god but God; the Sufi, the dervish, proclaims that only God *is*, that Reality itself, Being itself, is all and everything.

For the Sufi, then, monotheism, the proclamation of one God, is not confined to the corollary that no other gods exist. It also means that, despite appearances to the contrary, only God exists. This conviction does not mean that the appearance of separate beings is illusory; on the contrary, each being is real by virtue of being a manifestation of Being itself, of God Himself. But the apparent separation is apparent only, and all attempts to attain union with Being or God are futile: such union already obtains.

Thus the effort of the dervish is not to attain a state of being that already exists, but rather to recognize both the mistake in the sense of separation and the Reality of one's being a particle of the Divine. The waning of the former and the waxing of the latter depend upon remembering both truths.

Remembering God

The remembrance of God for the exoteric is a matter of performing prescribed rites, with or without an inward sense of intention. For the esoteric, it involves *zikhr*, a repetition of one or more of the names of God, similar in form to the mantra yoga of many Hindu paths.

The effort here is to cultivate concentrative attention by focusing on God, repeating God's name or names. In so doing, one forgets self and remembers God. Delving deeper, however, the effort involves remembering Self, one's authentic Identity.

Self-Remembering

The effort of self-remembering is more subtle, finer in quality, than the effort to remember God. One might gather that no effort could possibly be more subtle or finer than remembering God, but in remembering God and forgetting self one's authentic Self is also overlooked; one's Self is not included in the remembrance, so in fact one is not really remembering God on the deepest level. God is not completely included when one's Self is overlooked, forgotten.

Like the practice of *hitbonenuth* in the Jewish tradition, the practice of *zihkr* is deepest, most esoteric, when the Self is included. Without such an authentic Self-awareness, the practice of remembering God is a one way act of devotion, all of one's attention directed toward a separate God. Self-remembering, by contrast, recognizes the Condition of all conditions, the prior and always already Condition that is Being itself, Reality itself. Here God is no longer a separate being but one with the Self: nondual.

Thus the Sufi way demands an ever subtler effort as one develops the ability to join with the always already Reality, the Energy that is the greatness of God.

CHAPTER NINE

THE GURDJIEFF WORK

Gurdjieff's Way

George Gurdjieff was an Armenian-Greek teacher who during his youth traveled extensively throughout north Africa, the middle east, and Tibet, seeking the truth about reality. What he found, and what he formulated in a strikingly original way, was a teaching that antedated all the spiritual approaches we have considered in this book, a teaching independent of other lines or ways of working inwardly.

He began his teaching career in the early 20th century, in pre-revolutionary Russia, but had to leave Russia with his pupils as conditions became intolerable. He wound up in France, opening a school of inner work in a location near Paris. After a serious and almost fatal car accident Gurdjieff closed the school and began writing a series of books, a trilogy called *All and Everything*. During this period he also taught in a more informal way and commissioned elder students to conduct groups of their own. The end result of all this activity is that a Gurdjieff group exists in most major cities of the world, continuing the tradition that Gurdjieff initiated.

Initial Efforts

For one just entering a house of work in the Gurdjieff tradition, initial efforts might seem ordinary, particularly the effort to come to some sort of intellectual understanding of Gurdjieff's ideas. Yet even at the inception of inner work the ideas are presented in such a way, and under such conditions, that they act as catalysts for development of being.

Rather than considering many ideas as examples, it would be better to confine our study to one idea, one that has a direct bearing on the question of effort: man cannot do.

A Mistaken Sense Of Agency

Gurdjieff taught that our sense of being an agent of change is mistaken, that in fact we can do nothing. Things happen according to outer circumstances and inner conditioning, and then after such happening we trick ourselves with the thought "I did that."

There are two mistakes in that thought: the first is a mistaken sense or feeling of 'I'; the second is a mistaken sense of doing, of agency. In fact there is no such agent of change and therefore no one to do anything. Our inner conditioning is such that we believe we have a real self or identity capable of real action. Both beliefs are false.

Challenging False Beliefs

This idea immediately challenges our false beliefs about who we are and what we can do. Far from merely learning the idea intellectually, the initial effort is to accept the challenge by seeing for oneself if it can be verified.

An authentic sense of self and agency is subtly introduced in the instruction to *see* for oneself. In accepting the challenge one is also instructed not to substitute a new belief for the old, mistaken belief, but to attend all body-mind manifestations, including actions, impartially, without judgment.

The instruction to observe one's manifestations, study them, is an example of "skillful means." We have been tricked into a mistaken sense of self and agency by family and society; in following school instructions and living school conditions, we are being tricked into sensing and living an authentic sense of self and agency.

Attention

The direct yet subtle instruction to study one's manifestations introduces attention as the authentic identity and the authentic agent. Feeling is gradually withdrawn from the content of consciousness and found to be primordially situated in what is senior to that content, the apparent faculty of mind that can see, watch that content: attention.

For the newcomer to inner work attention appears to be just another faculty of the mind; later, however, one understands it is not a faculty but Mind itself, Identity itself; one comes to feel more and more that attention is one's identity.

Higher Attention

Soon enough another, more subtle effort is required: attending attention itself. As attention is more and more recognized as one's identity, one also recognizes that attention swims in its own awareness, is always already aware of itself. With this recognition attention also refines itself, becomes finer, and so invites an even higher attention to descend and inhabit the body.

This higher attention is the Shakti we have encountered in other traditions, and this higher energy with its intelligence is the Master, the real Self. And with this discovery development begins in earnest.

Development Of Being

The effort to receive higher energy is a very subtle effort of submitting to it, allowing it to enter and transform us. Such new and vivid impressions of ourselves also serves to develop our being. Energetic deposits are made in the body until eventually it becomes possible to feel another life, an independent life, developing within, apart from yet still connected to the usual life of the body-mind.

This new life has a different center of gravity; whereas before one has been centered in the head or perhaps the solar plexus, now one is drawn to the *hara*, the abdomen, as the place to which the higher energy descends and from which it ascends.

Now begins a struggle between these two lives as one finds oneself positioned between them. The old life, the old man, centered usually in the head, lost in egoic thoughts and feelings, pushed and pulled by outer forces and inner conditioning, protecting and defending a false sense of self and agency, and the new life, the new man, centered in the abdomen, receiving impressions of higher self and agency, living an altogether different life. The effort is to remain attentive, in between these two lives, while continuing to receive the impressions that further one's development.

The Locus Of Freedom

Family and the holding culture condition us into believing that we are agents capable of free choice and action. The Gurdjieff teaching, in concert with other authentic spiritual traditions, insists that freedom lies in an agency and an act anterior to what is normally conceived as free will or choice, a freedom to attend. The locus of freedom is in the attention.

For a considerable portion of the scientific community, and for the two major schools of psychology, free will, the freedom of choice, is an illusion; they agree with spiritual teachings that we have been tricked by our conditioning into believing we are agents of change. Determined completely by motivations and other features of our conditioning, no room remains for freedom; every effect has a cause, and every choice we think we make, every action we undertake, is completely determined by prior causes. In the realm of psychology such causes are called motivations.

Attention, when it is recognized at all by science, by scientific psychology, is treated as just another faculty of the mind. Gurdjieff, and other spiritual teachers, locate not only identity but also freedom in the attention. Attention, then, is not a faculty pertaining to the body-mind complex but is the only locale of identity and freedom. And it is only through attention that we can exercise something akin to free choice and free agency. All other manifestations are indeed determined.

A More Subtle Effort

The effort needed to verify the truth of attention's freedom is more subtle still than initial efforts in a given house of work in the Gurdjieff tradition. Even the rather pedestrian fact that one is free to direct one's attention is not familiar to most people; it is just done automatically, most often the attention being attracted rather than directed.

So first a given aspirant gains greater familiarity with freedom in the exercise of attention by struggling against conditioned manifestations, or, more fundamentally, by being reminded to awaken to one's freedom in the moment. Whether working with others on a craft project, moving with others in a movements class, or sitting with others in meditation, one verifies that there is a distinct threshold crossed from sleep, where one's attention is unrecognized and so one's false identity and mistaken sense of agency reigns, to awakening, where one's attention is recognized as one's real identity and one's actual sense of agency obtains.

A Most Subtle Effort

The effort to locate one's true feeling of identity and agency is difficult enough, but the effort to invite, to welcome, the higher attention from above is more subtle still, for it requires a complete divestment, in the moment, of the old feeling of self and the old feeling of agency. The effort involved approaches, as if to a mathematical limit, no effort at all. It is so subtle, so counterintuitive, as to be almost, yet not quite, impossible. It demands a profound inner stillness.

Gurdjieff introduced sacred dances or movements, and during such movements someone in authority might cry "Stop!" Dancers were expected to freeze in whatever position they happened to be in and observe all contents of consciousness. It was called the "stop exercise." In this exercise is a clue, and perhaps a foreshadowing, of the most subtle effort of all.

In another tradition, Vedanta, Ramana advised his listeners to "be still," and one of his devotees who went on to teach, Poonja, advised his pupils to "do nothing, just be quiet." In order to invite the energy from above the head, one must be still and do nothing, if by "doing" is meant ordinary efforts to attain this or that outcome.

Doing Nothing

Still, something must be done, and this is that most subtle of efforts; it amounts to not doing in the ordinary sense. But we have already seen that there is no real doing in this ordinary sense of the word, that egoic "doing" or agency is completely determined and so not real doing at all.

The admonition to stop, be still, and do nothing, is the demand to stop making egoic efforts. That is why it is imperative first to discover the locus of freedom, of real agency, in an action anterior to all other manifestations, in the attention, an attention freed from all motivation and so freed to welcome the real Agent of change.

Storming Heaven's Gates

Any other approach to spiritual development is a maladroit attempt to storm the gates of heaven through egoic efforts. The most subtle effort is the lightest touch, the most gentle allowing, conceivable.

We have already driven back a recognition of attention time and again through a misguided attempt to attain spiritual objectives. What is needed instead is a seeing without motive, without expectation of any result whatsoever. The conditioning, the ego, will doubtless want an outcome, will desire the higher as it desires any other object. But attention is capable of rising above all such desires, capable of action freed of all motivation for a desired outcome.

Real Doing

This freedom from motivation creates the possibility for real doing, authentic agency. Real doing is this most subtle of efforts. There is a saying in the Gurdjieff Work, "an effortless effort." It is a measure of our conditioning that the emphasis in that phrase usually falls on the word effort rather than on the word effortless. Properly understood, an effortless effort is no effort at all, at least as effort is understood by the holding culture.

An effortless effort is a complete stop. Such an effort calls off the search, as the search is often understood even in spiritual circles. Such an effort is stillness itself, a waiting upon the Lord, a silent welcoming to a higher force that is then disposed to descend. But first the body-mind must surrender its willful ways, its desire for attainment, in favor of a still, silent, stopped attentiveness.

Trying

Perhaps the most difficult, and trying, lesson to be learned in this and other spiritual ways of liberation is that the ego is an activity of avoidance, of escape from reality, and that because of that it can never approach the egoic goal of attaining liberation, enlightenment, or simply evolved being. Yet initial efforts have to begin with *trying* various methods, using assigned exercises for example, in order eventually to come to the realization that the activity we call ego is always and only an avoidance of what is, of Being itself. Egoic activity, trying various spiritual exercises or methods, can never attain its objective.

In the Gurdjieff Work this activity, especially in the initial stages of work, is conceived as ways to remind one to remember the Self, particularly during engagement with ordinary life. Many years may pass before one finally realizes that such methods will not work, and that moments of authentic Self-remembering come from above, not from below; higher energy, after sufficient deposits, calls one to itself, to what is in the moment. We do not, and cannot, remember; we *are* remembered.

Yet all this activity is part of being weaned from mistaken identity and agency and introduced to authentic identity and agency. Where can one begin except by exercising effort in the way one has been conditioned? So it is that exercises are provided, methods introduced, as ways that the aspirant can begin engaging the given spiritual path or way, exercises that after a certain time start to frustrate the usual way of trying to do on the deepest level. And what is usually frustrated in the Gurdjieff line of work is the mistaken belief that eventually one will be able to remember oneself continually, "always and everywhere."

Our real identity, our attention, is a ray of that divine awareness that alone is the authentic Agent of change. Yet the attention that we can work with and that has the possibility of being free of the activity of ego is very weak. To be sure, it can be developed, strengthened, but for the purpose not of working unaided but in order freely to receive needed help from above. The free act of remembering is initiated from another level altogether. Self-remembering, as Gurdjieff conceived it, is initiated by the authentic Self, the real Agent of change.

The Work Of Being

A given spiritual way is intended to bring the ongoing, always already work of Being into consciousness. Being, the Self, is always already adopting the role of a given finite perspective in a given human being, but this higher awareness is not known or understood by the person.

Once embarking upon a spiritual path, Being begins to make itself felt more and more to a given individual, while the person, as egoic activity, does his level best to avoid Being. Gradually the person comes to understand all activity as avoidance; even his attempts at spiritual exercises, though necessary, work as obstacles to the advent of Being. He is continually moving away while Being is continually moving toward. The only way for the individual to welcome Being is to come to a complete stop. And remain still.

All dreams of a continual Presence must also be dropped in this stop. All fantasies of attainment, enlightenment. A complete sacrifice of egoic activity. From that time forward, the authentic Agent of change will direct one's step along the path.

Developed Being

The Gurdjieff way is like Taoism, and unlike Vedanta and Buddhism, in its emphasis upon the evolution or development of being rather than enlightenment. Like Taoism, the interest is in creating a "soul."

This development depends upon the reception and assimilation of the energies of Being, and there is a reciprocal relationship between the discovery of Being and the development of being. Being must be discovered before development can proceed in earnest, and the more being is developed, the more Being can be recognized and so received.

The "state" or condition of enlightenment, as taught by Buddhism for example, is Being itself, Reality itself, always already the case. A certain development is usually needed to make this discovery, and, once made, development continues, only augmented, amplified, by the recognition of the Condition of all conditions, the State inclusive of all states. The ongoing recognition of what is, of Reality, replaces former efforts to find a state of being that can only be impermanent, and so not Reality itself.

CHAPTER TEN

THE SICKNESS OF EFFORT

Effort is the way;
Effort is the obstacle.

Sri Aurobindo

Effort Is The Way

We are so thoroughly conditioned by the holding culture that effort is required in order to begin challenging that conditioning with its mistaken thoughts and beliefs about who we are and what we can do. In this regard effort is indeed the way to our discovery of Being and from there its continued reception and assimilation.

We have seen repeatedly, by examining several spiritual ways or traditions, how initial stages of effort most resemble what we have learned about making efforts and attaining goals. So naturally we approach a spiritual way of life in the only way we know: making tense, muscular efforts in order to attain some goal, perhaps liberation, enlightenment, or simply greater being. Yet we have also seen how these spiritual ways begin subtly challenging this kind of effort right away, usually through both ideas and disciplines or exercises called *sadhana*, spiritual or inner work.

Spiritual methods or exercises are intended to introduce the aspirant to the seniority of attention, making possible the eventual discovery of unchanging silence or stillness. At the same time, there is a certain dynamism to be discovered, an energy accompanying the stillness, married to it, so to say. Several traditions symbolize this marriage as the embrace of Shiva and Shakti, the stillness of awareness with the energy of awareness.

Both stillness and energy comprise awareness, what has been called a dynamic stillness.

These discoveries initiate an altogether new kind of effort, one that recognizes the significance of both stillness and energy. The demand is for a more subtle effort, less willful, more submissive, more humble, a receptivity that acknowledges the indispensable role of awareness itself to the attainment of whatever goal one had originally envisioned for oneself.

The transition to a more subtle effort, however, takes some time to establish more than just a beachhead within a given individual's way of working. Even after one is introduced to the higher attention needed to develop being, the habits of a lifetime, perhaps of many lifetimes, remain firmly entrenched against any advances from above. The activity that is the ego does not easily raise the white flag of surrender. And only in a moment of surrender can the higher energy effect inner change.

Effort Is The Obstacle

Soon enough effort, so necessary in initial stages of inner work, becomes the chief obstacle to further development, for it comprises an essential part of what must be surrendered: the activity that *is* the ego.

Recall that this activity is an escape, an avoidance of Reality, of what is. All effort, all attempts to *do* something, is an avoidance, a turning of one's back, an effort to flee, what is here and now. Our conditioning is such that we would rather be anywhere but here, and at any time but now. Yet such activity, such effort, is futile, for we can be nowhere but here, and never be at any other place in time but now. We are always trying to avoid the present, but it is impossible to do so.

The effort, the activity, that is the ego relies for its survival on the illusion that escape is possible. For such activity cannot escape the eternal present, and yet it is always trying to do so. Spiritual exercises are given in order to drag this activity out into the open, from the shadows of ignorance into the light of knowledge. Spiritual methods are not given to attain anything, although the nascent aspirant can find no other meaning to them, given that the aspirant is still firmly in the grip of the ongoing activity of avoiding, of moving away from the real.

Such activity is only relatively real: it is real insofar as it, like all manifestation, is dependent for its being on the real; it is only relatively real insofar as it is founded upon, and rooted in, ignorance and illusion, the illusion that avoidance is even possible.

Spiritual Materialism

An important part of the spiritual materialism that Trungpa used to teach and write about is the effort to attain something as a result of "trying" or "doing" spiritual methods or exercises. No matter how many times a given individual is told not to work for results, the attempt to do so continues unabated, sometimes even while one is thinking one is *not* working for attainment. As long as one is *trying* to accomplish something, one is working toward a goal, an end, an objective; one is working for results.

It would seem, then, that it is impossible not to work for results, and so it is, provided one abides in the effort to *try* to do something. Some of the directives given to an aspirant may appear to be free of that taint of "doing," but once the individual begins to engage the directive in the old way of making an effort by trying, one is still mired in false identity and a mistaken sense of effort. Yet the directive, far from hoping that the one so directed will "succeed" in doing something, is intended gradually to wean that one from the illusion that anything real can be accomplished by trying in the way one has been conditioned to do.

"I" Cannot Do

Eventually, after a considerable period of time, and usually after countless attempts to do the impossible, one finally gives up, recognizing that this ersatz "I" or identity cannot do anything. One realizes that authentic agency must consist in some other activity than the usual activity that is the ego, the mistaken sense of "I" or identity. And it is most important, at this juncture, that one not give up completely, not despair of any possibility of finding the real Agent of change, of doing.

What is not seen for quite some time, usually many years, is that in trying to do a given spiritual exercise one is actually avoiding reality.

One identifies oneself as a seeker of truth, and so the activity that is the ego survives even within protected spiritual conditions. Yet the search is ultimately transforming, for it finally comes to an end when it is at last understood that all effort, all trying, is an impossible attempt to avoid reality, relying upon an activity that believes it is an entity, a real I with real power to do, a real agent of change. One is at last prepared, and ready, to be still.

Stopping

The transformative search continues, along with efforts, but in an entirely unfamiliar and unknown way. All usual activity, all trying, must stop. Yet stopping, as with all other actions, is not something one can do, neither can one try to do it. As spiritual masters like Shankara have repeatedly told us, discovery and development, liberation and enlightenment, are not the result of any action that we can perform. They are the manifestations of knowledge, of understanding.

We must understand our condition, our situation. All movement of the mind, feeling, and body is a moving away, an avoidance, an escape. Whenever we make an effort in the usual way, we must understand that no real action is engaged, as no real agent is there to do anything; it is only the activity of avoidance that is the ego, the illusory entity or self, an activity that tricks itself into a false impression of selfhood and agency.

At the same time, we have ready access to the authentic Agent of change, and this access begins with the recognition that our attention, when recognized, can be free of determining influences, free to refine itself and receive the Master, the inner Guru, the higher awareness and energy that is the real I, the real Self. And it is this attention, this freedom, that alone can stop the activity of avoidance.

I Can Do

If by "I" I mean my attention, then I can do; I can not *try* to do, but actually do, for my freed attention is here, now, and effective in its work. Because it is only here and only now, it is free of the determining influences of egoic activity, the impossible attempt to escape reality, avoid what is here now. Understanding is required, because although everything is only here now without understanding the futile attempt to be elsewhere will continue unchallenged.

Understanding that my usual "I" is nothing, a nonentity, only an activity that is not real action at all, I am at last ready to receive help from above. And "above" includes my "ordinary" attention when it is freed by understanding, by knowledge. Yet such freed attention is only the first breath of a much greater Identity descending from above to bless and empower. That is the real Agent of change, the Awareness that has always been available but which, in my eagerness to avoid it and so survive as "I," has been ignored in ignorance.

Knowledge, understanding, freed attention, stops egoic "activity" and ushers in the always already stillness and energy of Being. All functions of the mind, feeling, and body are allowed to be as they are, to arise, abide, and disappear naturally, overseen by awareness. Thoughts, for example, will arise, abide a bit, and dissipate just as all other impermanent phenomena do. Such phenomena are a part of what is, so they are all accepted; nothing is avoided by the incessant activity that is the ego. So it is not the arising and falling away of manifestation that is stopped, but the activity of avoidance. It is the effective death of such activity, and so the death of ego.

The Death Of Ego

The effective death of ego ushers in the promise of immortality, the creation of a soul or second body that will survive the death of the first or physical body. Such is the effective work of the authentic Agent of change, the real I.

This transformation means that for the individual there is a needed development beyond that surveyed by modern developmental psychology. This further development is unknown outside of spiritual schools, and even some spiritual traditions do not appear to acknowledge it. In our study both Taoism and the Gurdjieff Work explicitly teach it, and it is interesting that in both this development of being is given paramount importance, unlike other traditions that give first place to liberation or enlightenment.

In some spiritual traditions enlightenment is considered to be an event that happens to the mind, and as such is an event of realization; in other traditions it is conceived as a recognition of a flow of force or higher energy through the body. And in still others it is conceived as equivalent to Reality itself, always already the case, just unrecognized due to ignorance. However it is conceived, it is apparent that in most individuals a certain development of being is needed before the enlightened, stateless state is revealed.

Discovery And Development

Discovery, whether of attention, higher energy, or enlightenment, is reciprocally related to development. It is impossible to determine which comes first, but clearly there must be enough development to make a discovery, and because of discovery further development is made possible. One supports the other.

The effort needed in order to support this process of discovery and development is itself unlikely to be discovered, much less developed, so long as the hegemony of egoic activity is unchallenged. Once challenged, the slow but steady process of transitioning to authentic activity can be engaged. And authentic activity, real agency or doing, is not in any respect effort as it is understood and practiced by the holding culture.

What Is Effort?

Authentic effort is an unknown force, unknown by egoic activity yet understood through discovery and development. Authentic effort is a gift from above – in Christian terms, grace.

In the Christian tradition much debate has raged through the centuries about the place of works as related to the gift of grace. So long as "works" was conceived as something a given Christian could "do," no reconciliation between works and grace was possible. Some theologians preferred to abandon the effort at reconciliation and came down either on the grace side or works side; others continued to grapple with the antinomy. The real solution is in understanding that there is no work apart from grace.

The key is in discovering the freedom possible in the human structure. We have determined that it is to be found in a freed attention. All notions of any other sort of freedom contribute to the ongoing illusion of an ersatz self engaged in putative actions; what is actually the case is the futile attempt by a nonentity to escape reality. Both science and metaphysic refute these notions of freedom.

Effort, then, is an action from above, an action that stops the impossible attempt to avoid reality. The initial discovery of a freed attention leads inexorably to the discovery of a Work of an unknown, yet strangely familiar, Agent.

What Is Work?

To ask what is Work is to inquire into the meaning of authentic effort. Once again we must confess our inability to know, if by knowledge we mean a subject knowing an object, knowing in the scientific or scholarly sense. There is, however, a way to understand Work.

Work can be understood only by standing under it, by receiving it in the tissues of the body, allowing it to open and transform. It can be understood only when one is stopped by its influence; without its conscious reception one is abandoned to the hopeless effort of avoiding Work, avoiding Reality itself.

The initiative is not up to us; that is not our place. Neither is effort itself. What is up to us is an "effort" of seeking designed to wean us from avoidance to stillness, from inauthentic activity to authentic activity, from a mistaken identity to Real I. This is the only balm, the only salve, for the sickness of effort.

Coda

Work is beyond the limits of the mind.
No concept can define It.
No effort can reach It,
And no effort can avoid It.
It is nondual, spontaneously accomplished.
And so, having overcome the sickness of effort,
One finds oneself in the natural state
Of enlightened Presence,
Effortlessly resting
In Work itself.

BIBLIOGRAPHY

Amis, Robin. *A Different Christianity.* State University of New York, Albany, 1995.

Applebaum, David. *The Interpenetrating Reality.* Peter Land, New York, 1988.

Bokser, Ben Zion. *The Jewish Mystical Tradition.* Pilgrim, New York, 1981.

Bryant, Gary. *Invicti Solis.* Balboa, Bloomington, 2015.

_____. *The Liberation of Thought.* Balboa, Bloomington, 2015.

Buber, Martin. *Eclipse of God.* Humanities, New Jersey, 1952.

Burckhardt, Titus. *Alchemy.* Element, Longmead, 1987.

_____. *Introduction to Sufism.* Thorsons, San Francisco, 1976.

Chetanananda, Swami. *Dynamic Stillness.* Rudra, Cambridge, 1973.

Cooper, David. *God Is A Verb: Kabbalah and the Practice of Mystical Judaism.* Riverhead, New York, 1997.

De Salzmann, Jeanne. *The Reality of Being.* Shambhala, Boston, 2010.

Dowman, Keith. *The Flight of the Garuda.* Wisdom, Somerville, 2003.

Eliade, Mircea. *Yoga*. Princeton, 1958.

Feuerstein, Georg. *Tantra: The Path of Ecstasy*. Shambhala, Boston, 1998.

_____. *Yoga*. Jeremy Tarcher, Los Angeles, 1989.

Frantzis, B.K. *The Great Stillness*. North Atlantic, Berkeley, 2001.

Frawley, David. *Vedantic Meditation*. North Atlantic, Berkeley, 2000.

Gurdjieff, G.I. *Beelzebub's Tales to His Grandson*. E.P. Dutton, New York, 1950.

Kaplan, Aryeh. *Jewish Meditation*. Schocken, New York, 1985.

_____. *Meditation and The Bible*. Samuel Weiser, York Beach, 1978.

Kaufmann, Walter. *Religions in Four Dimensions*. Reader's Digest, New York, 1976.

Keating, Thomas. *Open Mind, Open Heart*. Amity, New York, 1986.

Klein, Anne Carolyn. "Psychology, the Sacred, And Energetic Sensing" in *Buddhism and Psychotherapy Across Cultures*. Ed. Mark Unno. Wisdom, Boston, 2006.

Krishnamurti, Jiddu. *The Flame of Attention*. Harper & Row, San Francisco, 1984.

Lamp of Non-Dual Knowledge & Cream of Liberation. Trans. Swami Sri Ramanananda Saraswathi. World Wisdom, Bloomington, 2003.

Lao Tzu. *Tao Te Ching*. Trans. Gia-Fu Feng & Jane English. Vintage, New York, 1989.

Levy, John. *The Nature of Man According to The Vedanta*. Sentient, Boulder, 2004.

Mead, GRS. *The Doctrine of The Subtle Body in The Western Tradition*. Solog, Motcombe, 1919.

Nasr, Seyyed Hossein. *Knowledge and The Sacred*. State University of New York, Albany, 1989.

Nisargadatta, Sri Maharaj. *I Am That*. Acorn, Durham, 1973.

Norbu, Namkhai. *Dzogchen*. Snow Lion, Ithaca, 1996.

_____. *The Mirror*. Station Hill, Barrytown, 1996.

Pagels, Elaine. *Beyond Belief*. Vintage, New York, 2003.

Pennington, M. Basil. *Centering Prayer*. Image, New York, 1980.

Ramana, Shankara, and The Forty Verses. Intro. Alan Jacobs. Watkins, 2002.

Ravindra, Ravi. *Yoga and The Teaching of Krishna*. Theosophical, Adyar, 1998.

Ray, Reginald. *Secret of The Vajra World: The Tantric Buddhism of Tibet*. Shambhala, Boston, 2001.

Sangpo, Khetsun. *Tantric Practice in Nying-ma*. Snow Lion, Ithaca, 1982.

Schuon, Frithjof. *The Transcendent Unity of Religions*. Quest, Wheaton, 1984.

Segal, William & Mariella Bancou-Segal. *A Voice at The Borders of Silence*. Overlook, Woodstock, 2003.

Self-Liberation Through Seeing with Naked Awareness. Trans. John Reynolds. Snow Lion, Ithaca, 2000.

Smith, Huston. *The Illustrated World's Religions.* Harper, San Francisco, 1995.

Subramuniyaswami, Sivaya. *Merging with Shiva.* Himalayan Academy, India, 1999.

Talks with Ramana Maharshi. Inner Directions, Carlsbad, 2000.

The Heart of Awareness. Trans. Thomas Byrom. Shambhala, Boston, 2001.

The Inner Journey: Views from The Gurdjieff Work. Ed. Jacob Needleman. Morning Light, Sandpoint, 2008.

The Philokalia. Trans. G.E.H. Palmer, Philip Sherrard, Kallistos Ware. Faber & Faber, London, 1984.

The Way of A Pilgrim. Trans. Olga Savin. Shambhala, Boston, 2001.

Trungpa, Chogyam. *Cutting Through Spiritual Materialism.* Shambhala, Boulder, 1973.

Waite, Dennis. *Back to The Truth: 5000 Years of Advaita.* Mantra, Winchester, 2007.

Wangyal, Tenzin. *Wonders of The Natural Mind.* Snow Lion, Ithaca, 2000.

Watts, Alan. *Behold The Spirit.* Vintage, New York, 1971.

_____. *Myth and Ritual in Christianity.* Beacon, Boston, 1968.

_____. *The Supreme Identity.* Vintage, New York, 1972.

Yeshe, Lama. *Introduction to Tantra.* Wisdom, Boston, 1987.

ABOUT THE AUTHOR

Gary Bryant is an ordained priest, a hospice chaplain, and a lifetime student of the world's spiritual traditions. He has five masters degrees, having studied at Rice University, The University of Chicago, and Harvard University. Gary is also the author of two books published by Balboa Press, *Invicti Solis* and *The Liberation of Thought*. Those two books, along with *The Sickness of Effort*, form a trilogy designed to explore the universal search for liberation.

With 30 years experience in a form of spirituality called the Gurdjieff Work, Gary is authorized to establish and foster individuals and groups in that tradition.

He is also past President of the Prometheus Society, past Membership Officer of the Triple Nine Society, a current member of the on line Four Sigma Society, former associate of the International Society for Philosophical Enquiry (ISPE), and a former lifetime member of Mensa.

Gary enjoys participating in athletic activities with his wife, with whom he resides in the Houston metro area.

Printed in the United States
By Bookmasters